Shine On! Plus 4

Workbook

T0346866

Contents

OXFORD
UNIVERSITY PRESS

The News Room

1 Read and write the days of the week in order. Draw.

Friday   Monday   Saturday   Sunday
Thursday   Tuesday   Wednesday

MY WEEK

2 Read, look, and write *his* or *her*. Follow and write the answers.

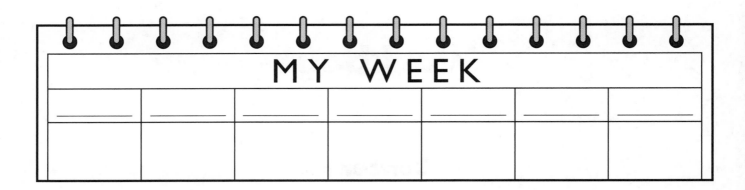

1 What's __her__ name?   Her name's Camila.   Eric

2 What's _____ name?   _____   Aliya

3 What's _____ name?   _____   Camila

4 What's _____ name?   _____   Tom

5 What's _____ name?   _____   Katie

6 What's _____ name?   _____   Lucas

1 Order the story. Read and circle.

What's **his / her** name?

His name's Matt.

Me too. But I **can / can't** read it.

And here are your **jobs / desks**! Welcome to the News Team. You're the Junior Crew.

Thanks!

What's her **name / job**?

She's a pilot! There's the news helicopter.

1 This is the news room.

Wow! An **astronaut / pilot**!

I have a **desk / message**.

Me too!

Sports News!

Lesson 1 **Story: Go Charlie!**

1 Look and read. Make a ✓ or an ✗.

① I can see a doctor. ✓

I can see a vet. ☐

I can see Amelia Angel. ☐

② I can see a bike. ☐

I can see a skateboard. ☐

I can see a surfboard. ☐

③ I can see Stella. ☐

I can see Joe. ☐

I can see Charlie. ☐

④ I can see three bikes. ☐

I can see a helicopter. ☐

I can see 10 people. ☐

1 Look, read, and write.

play soccer	skateboard
play volleyball	~~ride a bike~~
play baseball	surf
play tennis	play basketball

This is Samir. He can ¹ ___ride a bike___ ,
² _____ , ³ _____ ,
and ⁴ _____ .

This is Sara. She can ⁵ _____ ,
⁶ _____ , ⁷ _____ ,
and ⁸ _____ .

2 Write the questions in order. Look and write the answers.

1 she surf? Can

___Can she surf?___ ___Yes, she can.___

2 skateboard? he Can

_____ _____

3 soccer? Can she play

_____ _____

4 he play Can basketball?

_____ _____

5 play tennis? she Can

_____ _____

6 a bike? Can ride he

_____ _____

Vocabulary Sports **Grammar** Can she surf? Yes, she can. No, she can't.

1 Look, read, and write. Circle.

make   write   ride   take   draw

1 Can you _____ a bike?

 Yes, I can. / No, I can't.

2 Can you _____ videos?

 Yes, I can. / No, I can't.

3 Can you _____ photos?

 Yes, I can. / No, I can't.

4 Can you _____ pictures?

 Yes, I can. / No, I can't.

5 Can you _____ stories?

 Yes, I can. / No, I can't.

2 Follow and write the questions. Answer for you.

1 Can you draw pictures? _____

2 _____ _____

3 _____ _____

4 _____ _____

5 _____ _____

1 Look, read, and write.

beats   pulse   minute
seconds   heart rate

Lisa, let's take your ¹ _____ .

Give me your arm. First, let's count the

² _____ for 15 ³ _____ .

So, 4 x 33… your 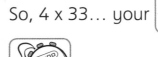 ⁴ _____ per

⁵ _____ is 132. That's very good!

2 Look, read, and match.

1 When I sleep, my heart rate is ●   ● 110 beats per minute.

2 When I walk, my heart rate is ●   ● 80 beats per minute.

3 When I skateboard, my heart rate is ●   ● 130 beats per minute.

4 When I play basketball, my heart rate is ●   ● 100 beats per minute.

1 Look, read, and write.

can   can't   well   very well   at all

I _____ skateboard _____ .

I _____ skateboard _____ .

I _____ skateboard _____ .

2 Read and circle. Answer for you.

1 Can you cook?

Yes, I can. / No, I can't.   _____

2 Can you dance?

Yes, I can. / No, I can't.   _____

3 Can you surf?

Yes, I can. / No, I can't.   _____

4 Can you sing?

Yes, I can. / No, I can't.   _____

5 Can you draw?

Yes, I can. / No, I can't.   _____

1 Look and write the questions.

What can you do?

		very well	well	not at all
⚽	**1** Can you surf?	☺	☺ ☺ ☺	☺ ☺ ☺ ☺ ☺ ☺
🏀	**2** _____	☺ ☺ ☺ ☺ ☺ ☺ ☺ ☺	☺ ☺	
🛹	**3** _____	☺ ☺	☺ ☺ ☺ ☺	☺ ☺ ☺
🚲	**4** _____	☺ ☺ ☺	☺ ☺ ☺ ☺ ☺ ☺	☺
🏐	**5** _____	☺ ☺ ☺ ☺	☺ ☺ ☺ ☺ ☺ ☺	
⚾	**6** _____	☺ ☺	☺ ☺ ☺	☺ ☺ ☺ ☺ ☺

2 Look at activity 1. Read and circle.

Hello. I'm Ahmed and I'm in class 4B.

In my class, **eight / two** students can play basketball very well.

Five students can **play volleyball / skateboard** well.

Six students can ride a bike **very well / well**, but six students can't **surf / skateboard** at all.

Two students can play baseball **very well / well** and **five / six** students can play volleyball well.

It's Showtime!

Lesson 1 | Story: Two New Dancers!

1 Look, read, and write.

> Yes, they are.   Stella can dance!   They're acrobats.
> They're reporters.   Are they dancers?   They aren't dancers!

①

Here are the Junior Crew!
_____

Welcome! It's the big night tonight!

②

Cool!
_____

No, they aren't.
_____

③

Are they artists?

_____

④

Come on! Hurry up! All dancers over here!

⑤

Hurry up!

Wait!
_____

They're reporters …

⑥

Hey! _____ She's fantastic!

Yes, but Lily can't!

2 Lesson 2

1 Find and circle. Look and write.

dfbuilderqisecretarysuedancervmwcleanerthkacrobatpzdirectordwartistjxnreportervoq

①  _____

② _____

③  _____

④  _____

⑤  _____

⑥  _____

⑦  _____

⑧  _____

2 Look, read, and write.

1 Are they dancers? <u>Yes, they are</u> .

2 _____ acrobats? _____ .

3 Are they artists? No, _____ . They're _____ .

4 _____ directors? _____ . _____ .

1 Look, read, and match.

1 Are they bored?

No, they aren't. They're proud. ●

2 Are they afraid?

Yes, they are. ●

3 Are they excited?

Yes, they are. ●

4 Are they proud?

No, they aren't. They're bored. ●

2 Write the questions and answers. Use *Yes, I am.* or *No, I'm not.*

1 **Reporter:** <u>Are you afraid?</u>   (afraid)

  Gabriel: _____

2 **Reporter:** _____ (bored)

  Anna: _____

3 **Reporter:** _____ (excited)

  Jacob: _____

4 **Reporter:** _____ (proud)

  Laura: _____

Vocabulary Feelings **Grammar** Are you afraid? No, I'm not. Yes, I am.

1 Look, read, and write.

> afraid   angry   happy
> sad   surprised   ~~tired~~

①  **+** ⌢ ___tired___

② 👀 **+** ⌢ _____

③ 👀 **+** ⌣ _____

④ 👀 **+** ◣ _____

⑤ 👀 **+** 😃 _____

⑥ 👀 **+**   _____

2 Look, draw, and write.

①    ②    ③

_He's_ _____.   _____   _____

Vocabulary tired, surprised, angry, afraid, sad, happy   **13**

1 Look, read, and number in order.

☐ And this photo? I think they're reporters.

☐ Yes, I think so, too.

☐ Look at this photo. I think they're dancers.

☐ Really? I don't think so. I think they're acrobats.

2 Look, read, and write.

at all   I think so, too   I think   I don't think so   very well

Look at this picture. ¹_____ he's a cleaner.

Really? ²_____. I think he's an artist.

Oh, yes, ³_____ . He can draw ⁴_____ .

I can't draw ⁵_____ !

1 Look, read, and number.

1 This is a great show! There are six acrobats and they're fantastic! They aren't afraid at all.

2 I can't wait to see this show! There are ten dancers. They can also sing and act. I'm very excited!

3 This is such a funny show! I'm not bored at all! There are eleven artists and they all work very hard. They're proud of the show.

2 Look at activity 1. Read and write.

dancers   director   aren't
It's   proud   They're

Hi! I'm Lisa and I'm at *Let's Dance!* There are six ¹_____ in the show. They ²_____ afraid. ³_____ excited! The ⁴_____ is my brother. I'm very ⁵_____ ! Come and see this show. ⁶_____ fantastic!

Revision 1

1 Look and write.

2 Look, read, and write. Match.

draw pictures   make videos   take photos   write stories

 1 I can _____ . ●   ● artist

 2 I can _____ . ●   ● builder

 3 I can _____ . ●   ● director

 4 I can _____ . ●   ● reporter

3 Write the questions in order. Look and write the answers.

1 ride a you bike? Can

_____

_____

2 surf? Can she

_____

_____

3 he play Can tennis?

_____

_____

4 you skateboard? Can

_____

_____

4 Read and follow. Circle and write.

1 Are **you** / **they** bored?

_____

2 Are **you** / **they** proud?

_____

3 Are **you** / **they** afraid?

_____

4 Are **you** / **they** excited?

_____

In the Ocean

Lesson 1 | **Story: Beach Rescue!**

1 Look, read, and answer.

No, they aren't.   No, they aren't.   Yes, it is.
No, it isn't.   ~~Yes, they are.~~   Yes, they are.

①

Are they seals?

Yes, they are.

②

Are they sharks?

_____

③

Are they afraid?

④

Is it happy?

_____

⑤

Is it OK?

⑥

Are they happy?

_____

3 Lesson 2

1 Read, look, and match.

1 fi   horse

2 wha   tle

3 sea   sh

4 tur   al

5 sha   phin

6 se   rk

7 dol   opus

8 oct   le

2 Look and write. Use *This is* or *These are*.

1 <u>This is an octopus.</u>

2 _____

3 _____

4 _____

5 _____

6 _____

1 Look, read, and write. Use *That's* or *Those are*. Then number.

1 What are those? _____ seals. They're funny.

2 What's that? _____ a whale. It's shy.

3 What are those? _____ seahorses. They're friendly.

4 What's that? _____ an octopus. It's smart.

2 Look and write questions and answers. Circle.

1 What are those? _Those are_ _____. They're **funny / shy**.

2 What's that? _____ It's **friendly / smart**.

3 _____ _____ They're **shy / funny**.

4 _____ _____ It's **smart / friendly**.

1 Look, read, and write.

beach   deep   ocean floor
rock pool   shallow

Ocean Habitats

2 _____

3 _____

_____

4 _____

5 _____

2 Look, read, and number. Write.

☐   ☐   ☐   ☐   ☐

1   They like the beach. They swim fast in the water, too. _____

2   They like the rock pools. _____

3   They swim in shallow waters on the ocean floor. _____,
     _____, and _____

4   They can go on the beach, but they like to swim in the ocean. _____

5   They swim in deep waters. _____, _____, and
     _____

1 Look, read, and write.

next   What   go   Let's   next

____ ____?

____ ____
and see the seals
____.

Good idea!

2 Look, read, and number in order.

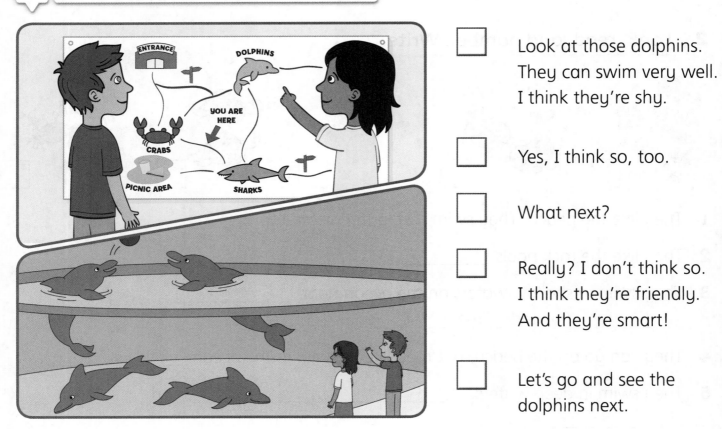

☐ Look at those dolphins. They can swim very well. I think they're shy.

☐ Yes, I think so, too.

☐ What next?

☐ Really? I don't think so. I think they're friendly. And they're smart!

☐ Let's go and see the dolphins next.

3 Lesson 6

1 Read, look, and make a ✓. Write.

Ocean Animals Quiz!

What animal is this?

1 This animal is big.

2 This animal is shy.

3 This animal likes the beach and water.

4 This animal has legs.

It's a _____!

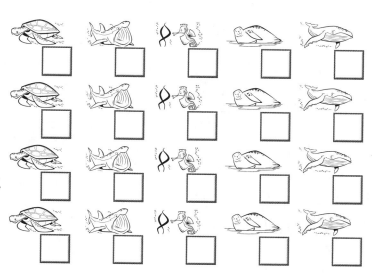

2 Look, read, and write.

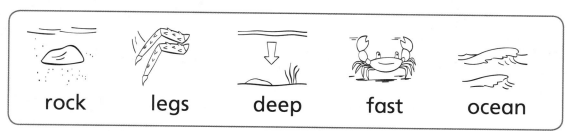

rock   legs   deep   fast   ocean

I'm a small, ¹ _____ animal. I don't like ² _____ water. I like shallow water and ³ _____ pools. I can walk ⁴ _____ and I can swim, but not very well. I have ten ⁵ _____. I'm a crab!

4 At the Fun Run!

Lesson 1 **Story: At the Fun Run**

1 Order the story. Write.

umbrella   costume   money   cap   medal   Amy

Thank you, Amy! Here's your _____.

Does she have an _____?

No, she doesn't. That isn't Amy.

There's Amy! She has an astronaut _____!

Cool! And there's her brother.

Does she have a pink _____?

No, she doesn't.

Wow! You have a lot of _____, Amy!

Yes! It's heavy!

I can't see _____.

Lesson 2

1 Look, read, and write.

backpack   cap   costume   ~~first aid kit~~
edal   money   umbrella   water bottle

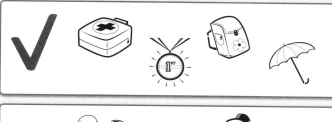

1 I have a ___first aid kit___,
a _____, a _____,
and an _____.

2 I don't have a _____,
a _____, a _____,
or _____.

2 Write. Use *Does he* or *Does she*. Look and write the answers.

1 ___Does he___ have a cap?   ___No, he doesn't.___

2 _____ have a first aid kit?   _____

3 _____ have an umbrella?   _____

4 _____ have a costume?   _____

5 _____ have money?   _____

6 _____ have a medal?   _____

Vocabulary Useful things **Grammar** Does he have a cap? Yes, he does. No, he doesn't.   25

1 Look, read, and circle.

① ✔ ②  ✘ ③  ✔ ④  ✔

Do you have an aunt?   Yes, I do. / No, I don't.

Do you have any cousins?   Yes, I do. / No, I don't.

Do you have an uncle?   Yes, I do. / No, I don't.

Do you have any friends?   Yes, I do. / No, I don't.

2 Look, read, and write.

What's your name?

My name's Carlos.

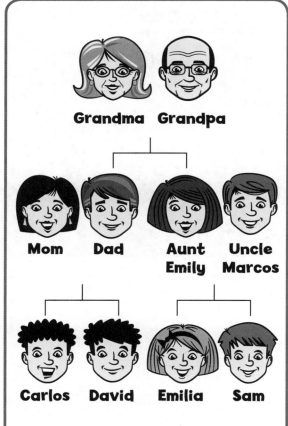

Grandma   **Grandpa**

Mom   **Dad**   **Aunt Emily**   **Uncle Marcos**

Carlos   **David**   **Emilia**   **Sam**

1 **Teacher:** <u>Do you have any brothers?</u> (brothers
   Simon: <u>Yes, I do.</u> I have one brother. His name's _____.

2 **Teacher:** _____ (sisters)
   Simon: _____.

3 **Teacher:** _____ (cousins)
   Simon: _____. I have two cousins. Their names are _____.

4 **Teacher:** _____ (uncles)
   Simon: _____. I have one uncle. His name's _____.

5 **Teacher:** _____ (aunts)
   Simon: _____. I have _____.

4 Lesson 4 | Science

1 Look and make a ✓ or an ✗. Read and write.

> Drink water.   Put on a cap.   Stretch.
> Take a break.   ~~Warm up your muscles.~~

①

Warm up your
muscles.

②

_____

③

_____
_____

④

_____
_____

⑤

_____
_____

2 Look at activity 1. Read and write.

Safe Sports

1 Warm _up your muscles_. Walk for five minutes.

2 Stay cool when you jog. Put on
a _____.

3 _____ water. Do you have a
water bottle?

4 Take a _____. Have a healthy snack.

5 _____ your arms and legs after sports.

1 Look, read, and write. Match.

> bike and a kite   present and a card
> backpack and a water bottle

①

Let's go to the party.

What shall I bring?

Bring a _____.

②

Let's go to the park.

What shall I bring?

Bring a _____.

③

Let's go to the mountain.

What shall I bring?

Bring a _____.

2 Read and number in order. Look and draw.

☐ Yes, I can surf very well.

☐ Bring a cap and a sandwich.

☐ Can you surf?

☐ Really? OK. Let's go to the beach.

☐ What shall I bring?

1 Read, look, and match.

①  Grandpa Tom ●

②   Cousin Annie ●

③   Uncle Steve ●

④   Aunt Mary ●

Today is the *Fun Run!* The run is for my school. Aunt Mary and Uncle Steve are there. Aunt Mary has a firefighter costume and Uncle Steve has an octopus costume. He's very funny! Grandpa Tom has a builder costume. My cousin Annie is there, too! She has a seahorse costume.

2 Look, read, and circle. Write *has* or *doesn't have*.

1 He / She _____has_____ a first aid kit.

2 He / She _____ a backpack.

3 He / She _____ an umbrella.

4 He / She _____ a water bottle.

My **aunt / cousin / grandpa / uncle** has the medal! Good job!

Revision 2

1 Look, read, and write.

a e i o u

1 The f __ sh are fr __ __ ndly.

2 The wh __ l __ is shy.

3 The s __ __ h __ rs __ s are f __ nny.

4 The __ ct __ p __ s is sm __ rt.

2 Look, unscramble the words, and write.

①

o s
c t m
u e

_____

②

d a
m l e

_____

③

d k f
a i i t
s t i r

_____

④

p c a

_____

⑤

e n
m y o

_____

3 Look and write. Use *this*, *these*, *that*, and *those*.

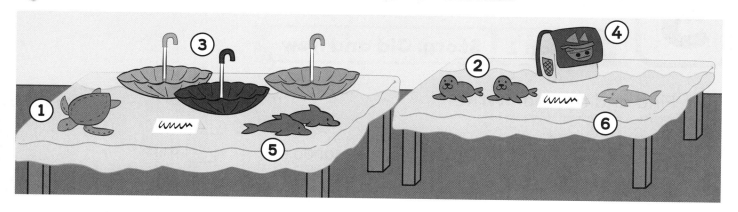

1 What _'s that_____? _____That's_____ a turtle.

2 What _____? _____ seals.

3 What _____? _____ umbrellas.

4 What _____? _____ a backpack.

5 What _____? _____ dolphins.

6 What _____? _____ a shark.

4 Write the questions. Look and write the answers.

1 _Do you have a cousin_____? (you / cousin) _____

2 _____? (she / aunt) _____

3 _____? (he / water bottle) _____

4 _____? (you / umbrella) _____

5 _____? (she / backpack)   _____

At the Fashion Show

Lesson 1 | **Story: Old and New**

1 | Find and number. Write.

| hat | 1 dress | sandals | shirt |
| scarf | leggings | jeans | coat |

Oh! She isn't wearing a pink ___dress___.

Look! She's wearing _____.

Wow! He's wearing a cool _____ and _____!

Thank you everyone! And thank you Stella!

Old _____ are cool now!

1 Look, read, and write.

| jeans | sneakers | leggings | coat | sandals | shirt | scarf | dress |

① _____

② _____

③ _____

④ _____

⑤ _____

⑥ _____

⑦ _____

⑧ _____

2 Look, color, and write. Use *is wearing* or *isn't wearing*.

Nick   Eva

▲ orange
■ red
◆ blue
● purple
♠ brown
⬡ green

Eva

1 She __'s wearing__ a blue dress.

2 _____ a yellow scarf.

3 _____ brown sandals.

Nick

4 _____ red jeans.

5 _____ green sneakers.

6 _____ a black shirt.

Vocabulary Clothes **Grammar** She isn't wearing a pink dress. She's wearing a blue dress.

1 | Read, look, and match.

1 Look at John.
He's wearing a watch. ●

Look at Sarah.
She's wearing a belt. ●

2 Look at John now.
He's wearing sunglasses. ●

Look at Sarah now.
She's wearing gloves. ●

2 | Read and write questions and answers. Draw.

① 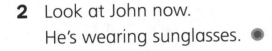 What's she wearing?

__She's wearing a watch.__

(a watch)

② What's he _____ ?

_____

(sunglasses)

③  _____

_____

(a belt)

④  _____

_____

(gloves)

1 Read, look, and write.

design   made of   recycle   trash can

1 Don't put your old things in the _____ .

2 You can _____ them and make new things.

3 You can _____ really cool things! This rug is

 _____ old T-shirts.

2 Read, look, and match.

1 I can sit on it.

2 I can play with it.

3 I can put my pencils and crayons in it.

4 I can wear them.

They're made of old trash.

It's made of old socks.

It's made of old jeans.

It's made of old bottles.

1 Look, read, and match.

①

Really? I prefer this belt!

②

I love these sunglasses.

③

I love these gloves.

2 Look, read, and number in order.

☐ Yes, I think so, too. I love green.

☐ Look at this picture. I think she's wearing leggings.

☐ Really? I prefer blue.

☐ I don't think so. I think she's wearing green pants.

1 Look, read, and circle.

Hannah can play soccer very well. She has a **stylish / sporty** look! She's wearing her new **sneakers / sandals** and fun **jeans / leggings**. Look at her **shirt / T-shirt**. It has a soccer ball on it. Cool!

2 Look and draw. Write.

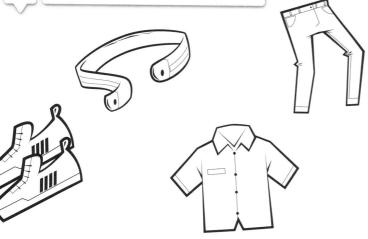

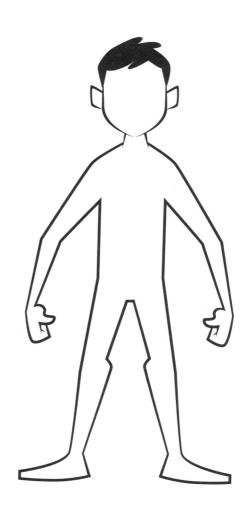

1 <u>He isn't wearing a scarf.</u> (scarf)

2 _____ (jeans)

3 _____ (a belt)

4 _____ (gloves)

5 _____ (sneakers)

6 _____ (a shirt)

At the Wildlife Club

1 Look and read. Make a ✓ or an ✗.

①

I can see a helicopter. ☐

I can see a lake. ☐

I can see a plane. ☐

②

I can see artists. ☐

I can see reporters. ☐

I can see builders. ☐

③

I can see a squirrel. ☐

I can see a rabbit. ☐

I can see a frog. ☐

④

I can see four children. ☐

I can see two flowers. ☐

I can see two foxes. ☐

6 Lesson 2

1 Find and circle. Write.

awbuildgsdrinkhueatialistenftreadbjsleepxjwalkefwatchse

1 _____

2 _____

3 _____

4 _____

5 _____

6 _____

7 _____

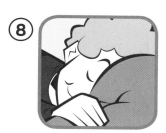
8 _____

2 Look, read, and write.

1

2

3

4

1 They aren't watching.   They're _____ .

2 _____   They're drinking.

3 They aren't reading.   _____

4 _____   They're sleeping.

Vocabulary Actions **Grammar** They aren't watching. They're drinking.   39

6 Lesson 3

1 Read, follow, and write.

quarter to twelve   four thirty
ten thirty   quarter to one
six o'clock   two o'clock

What time is it?

1 It's _____ .

2 It's _____ .

3 It's _____ .

4 It's _____ .

5 It's _____ .

6 It's _____ .

2 Look, read, and write.

1 They're sleeping. What time is it?

   It's _____ .

2 They're drinking. What time is it?

   It's _____ .

3 They're watching. What _____ ?

   _____

4 They're eating. _____ ?

   _____

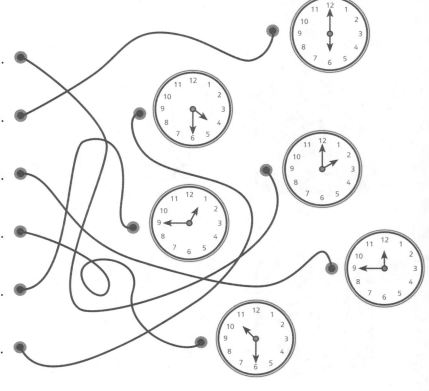
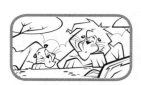

Vocabulary Time **Grammar** What time is it? It's quarter to two.

1 Look, read, and write.

fall spring summer winter

1 _____

2 _____

3 _____

4 _____

2 Read, look, and circle. Write.

Bears Through the Seasons

1 It's ___summer___. It's hot. The young bears are _____.

2 It's _____. The bears are awake. They're _____.

3 It's _____. It's cold. They're _____.

4 It's _____. The bears are busy. They're _____.

1 Look, read, and write.

I'm at the toy store.   What are you up to?
I'm playing tennis.

①

②

2 Look, read, and write.

at all   playing   bring   let's go

Samir: Hi, Sam. What are you up to?

Caleb: I'm ¹_____ baseball.

Samir: Really? Can you play baseball?

Caleb: No, I can't play baseball ²_____ .
I'm bored!

Samir: Well, ³_____ to the park!

Caleb: OK. What shall I ⁴_____?

Samir: Bring your scooter and a ball.

Caleb: OK!

1 Look, read, and write.

~~build~~ climb eat play sleep walk

Jayla's Wildlife Watch!

There are two funny animals in my yard. They're hedgehogs! Look what they're doing.

1 It's six o'clock in the morning. They're ___building___ their home.

2 It's nine thirty now. Be quiet. They're _____ .

 **3** It's quarter to five. They're _____ with my toys!

4 They're _____ on my sneakers! It's quarter past six.

 **5** They're _____ in the yard. It's eight o'clock.

6 It's eight thirty. They're _____ grass and mushrooms. They're hungry!

2 Look at activity 1. Read and draw.

1 They're climbing.

2 They're playing.

3 They're building.

4 They're sleeping.

5 They're eating.

6 They're walking.

Revision 3

1 Look and write.

1 d _ _ _ _ _ _

Clothes

5 b _ _ _ _

4 c _ _ _ _

2 j _ _ _ _ _ _

Accessories

6 g _ _ _ _ _ _ _

8 s _ _ _ _ _ _ _ _ _ _ _

3 s _ _ _ _ _

7 w _ _ _ _ _

2 Look, unscramble the words, and write.

①

e l i n s t

_____

②

d b i l u

_____

③

a w k l

_____

④

n r i d k a e t

_____

⑤

a r e d t c w h a

_____

3 Look, read, and write. Use *'s wearing* or *isn't wearing*.

Claire

1 Look at Claire. What's she wearing? <u>She isn't wearing sneakers.</u>

2 Look at her dad. What's he wearing? _____

3 Look at her grandpa. What's he wearing? _____

4 Look at her mom. What's she wearing? _____

5 Look at her brother. What's he wearing? _____

6 Look at her grandma. What's she wearing? _____

4 Look, read, and follow. Write.

1 `7:45` It's <u>quarter to eight.</u>
They're <u>drinking juice.</u>

 eat a sandwich

2 `3:00` It's _____
They're _____

 walk home

3 `7:15` It's _____
They aren't _____

 read a book

4 `8:30` It's _____
_____

 drink juice

5 `5:00` It's _____
_____

 sleep

6 `6:30` It's _____
_____

 watch TV

The Open Day

1 Check (✓) the places in the story. Write.

☐ the science room   ☐ the music room   ☐ the art room

✓ the geography room   ☐ the PE room   ☐ the math room

the geography room

_____

_____

_____

2 Remember the story. Circle the mystery animal.

mouse   chicken   monkey   fox

1 Look, unscramble the words, and write.

	Monday			Tuesday	
①	👑	tyiorhs <u>history</u>	⑤	🌐	apoegrhyg _____
②	🏀	EP _____	⑥	🎵	scumi _____
③	📖	glEsinh _____	⑦	✕ ÷ +	ahtm _____
④	🧪	cceeisn _____	⑧	✏️	rta _____

2 Look and write. Use *likes* or *doesn't like*.

1 She <u>likes music</u> and <u>science</u> .

2 She _____ or _____ .

3 He _____ or _____ .

4 He _____ and _____ .

7 Lesson 3

1 Read, match, and write.

1 He likes  . ●

2 She likes  . ●

3 He likes ⚹ . ●

4 She likes 🥋 . ●

●

●

_____

● _____

●

_____

2 Look and write questions and answers.

Simon

Alisha

Simon

1 Does he like math?

   Yes, he does.

2 _____

   _____

3 _____

   _____

Alisha

4 _____

   _____

5 _____

   _____

6 _____

   _____

Vocabulary Activities **Grammar** Does he like math? Yes, he does. No, he doesn't.

1 Look, read, and write.

| groups   in common   rule   Venn diagram |

1 This is a _____ .

2 There are three _____ .

3 Three students have something
   _____ .

4 We can make this _____ :
   three students like science and English.

2 Read and draw ☺ in the Venn diagram.

There are 15 students in my class.

Five students like PE and music.

Four students like PE.

Three students like music.

Two students like geography and PE.

One student likes PE, geography, and music.

1 | Look and write the words in order.

①

②

art I'm at good

Harry: _____

at good I'm music not

Mia: _____

2 | Read. What's Helen good at? Look and make a ✓ or an ✗.

Sofia: Let's go to the park!

Helen: OK. What shall we play?

Sofia: Baseball!

Helen: Sorry, I'm not good at baseball.

Sofia: Can you play tennis?

Helen: No. I can't play tennis at all.

Sofia: Can you play basketball?

Helen: No. I don't think so. I'm good at soccer!

Sofia: OK. Let's go and play soccer!

①

②

③

④

7 Lesson 6

1 Look and read. Write the names.

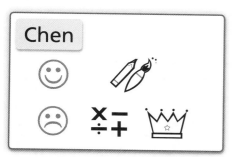

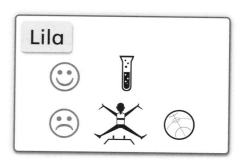

1 Hi! I'm _____ . My favorite subjects are English and geography. I don't like music. I can't sing at all!

2 My name is _____ . I like art. I can draw very well. I don't like history or math.

3 Hello. I'm _____ . I'm not good at sports so I don't like PE or gymnastics. My favorite subject is science.

2 Look at activity 1. Write the questions and circle the answers.

1 Roberto 🌐

  Does Roberto like geography?   Yes, he does. / No, he doesn't.

2 Lila 🧪

_____ Yes, she does. / No, she doesn't.

3 Chen 👑

_____ Yes, he does. / No, he doesn't.

4 Lila 🏀

_____ Yes, she does. / No, she doesn't.

5 Roberto 🎵

_____ Yes, he does. / No, he doesn't.

6 Chen ×−÷+

_____ Yes, he does. / No, he doesn't.

Are You Hungry?

Lesson 1 | **Story: The Cooking Contest**

1 Look, read, and write the missing letters.

① A contest! Let's do it!

Great. I love p _i_ z _z_ a!

② OK, we need t _ m _ t _ e _ .

And we need c h _ _ s _ .

③ We need p _ p _ e _ s.

And we need o _ i _ e _ .

④ What are these?

Those are c _ i _ i _ e _ p _ r _ .

2 Read and number.

☐ Lily has cheese.

☐ Charlie likes pizza.

☐ It's twelve o'clock.

☐ They need peppers.

1 Look, count, and write the number. Write for you.

1 chili peppers ☐   5 peppers ☐

2 mushrooms ☐   6 potatoes ☐

3 olives ☐   7 sausages ☐

4 onions ☐   8 tomatoes ☐

☺ I like...

☹ I don't like...

2 Look and write. Use *We need* or *We don't need*.

1 <u>We need eight chili peppers.</u>

2 <u>We don't need potatoes.</u>

3 _____

4 _____

5 _____

6 _____

7 _____

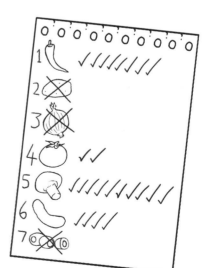

1 What's next? Look and draw. Then read and write the answers.

1

Do you need jelly? _____

2

Do you need bread? _____

3

Do you need ham? _____

4

Do you need butter? _____

2 Look and write.

1 <u>Do you need jelly?</u>
  <u>Yes, I do.</u>

2 _____
  _____

3 _____
  _____

4 _____

5 _____
  _____

Vocabulary Food **Grammar** Do you need jelly? Yes, I do. No, I don't.

1 Read, write, and match.

bones   building blocks   energy
muscles   treats   vitamins

1 Chicken is good for our _____. ●

2 Ice cream and candy are _____. ●

3 Bread gives us _____. ●

4 Olives and butter help make the
_____ of the body. ●

5 Cheese makes our _____ strong. ●

6 Tomatoes and peppers give us _____. ●

2 Look at activity 1. Read and write.

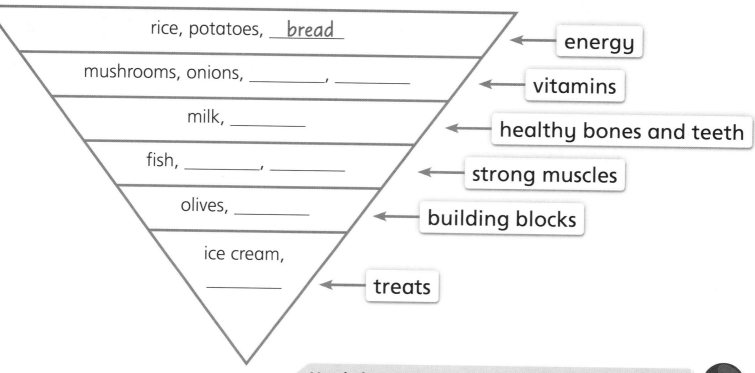

rice, potatoes, _bread_ ← energy

mushrooms, onions, _____, _____ ← vitamins

milk, _____ ← healthy bones and teeth

fish, _____, _____ ← strong muscles

olives, _____ ← building blocks

ice cream, _____ ← treats

1 Look, read, and number.

1 Here you go. Anything else? **2** We need tomatoes. **3** That's all, thanks!

2 Look, read, and write.

> all   anything   here   love   next   really

①

Sophie: I ¹_____ chili peppers.

Amir: ²_____? I prefer these peppers.

Sophie: OK.

②

Sophie: Hello. We need peppers, please.

Natalia: OK. ³_____ you go. ⁴_____ else?

Amir: I don't think so. That's ⁵_____, thanks!

Natalia: You're welcome.

Amir: What's ⁶_____, Sophie? What shall we buy?

Sophie: Let's go and get bread.

1 Look and read. Number.

Zoe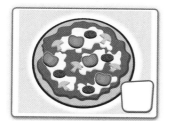

① For this pizza, we don't need tomatoes or onions. We need sausages and chili peppers. Yum!

Hugo ②

Here's my favorite pizza! To make it, we need peppers, mushrooms, and onions. We don't need sausages.

Celia ③

My pizza recipe is great! We need mushrooms and tomatoes. Oh, and sausages. We don't need peppers.

2 Look at activity 1. Read, write, and circle.

1 Do you need mushrooms? No, I _____.   Hugo / Zoe

2 Do you need tomatoes? Yes, I _____.   Celia / Zoe

3 Do you need onions? No, I _____.   Zoe / Hugo

4 Do you need sausages? No, I _____.   Hugo / Zoe

5 Do you need chilli peppers? Yes, I _____.   Zoe / Celia

6 Do you need peppers? Yes, I _____.   Hugo / Celia

Revision 4

1 Read, unscramble the words, and write. Match.

School Subjects and Activities

1 I like _____ i o s r h t y ●

2 I don't like _____ c n i e c s e ●

3 I like _____ t m h a ●

4 I don't like _____ m i g n a s c y t s ●

Food

5 I don't like _____ s s a g u e a s ●

6 I like _____ p p e e r p s ●

7 I don't like _____ o i o s n n ●

8 I like _____ o t o t a p e s ●

2 Look and write for you.

School Subjects and Activities	Food
I like	I like
I don't like	I don't like

3 Look, read, and write. Use *likes* or *doesn't like*.

This is my friend, Elsa. She ¹_____ 🎵.

This is her favorite subject. She ²_____

✏️, too. She ³_____ 🏀. Elsa

⁴_____ 🪣. She ⁵_____ 🎱!

4 Look at activity 3. Write questions and answers.

1 Does Elsa like music?   Yes, she does.

2 Does she like art?   _____

3 _____   _____

4 _____   _____

5 _____   _____

5 Write the questions in order. Look and write the answers.

1 you Do tomatoes? need
   Do you need tomatoes?   Yes, I do.

2 need you olives? Do
   _____   _____

3 chili Do need you peppers?
   _____   _____

4 sausages? Do need you
   _____   _____

Popular Sports

1 Look, read, and circle.

team / player

hockey / football

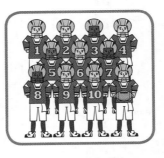

team / player

hockey / football

2 Look, read, and write.

①  Ben

I play _____ at school, but I don't play in a _____ . I can throw the ball and catch it. I can run fast, too. Playing this sport makes me happy!

②  Hayley

I like sports. I can play basketball well, but my favorite sport is _____ ! I'm a _____ for the *Super Skaters* at school. All the other players are my friends.

3 Look at activity 2. Read and write.

1 Can Hayley play two sports well?   <u>Yes, she can.</u>

2 Can Ben play football well?   _____

3 Is Hayley on a hockey team?   _____

4 Is Ben on a football team?   _____

5 Are Hayley and Ben excited about sports?   _____

Vocabulary hockey, football, team, player

Out in the Wild

1 Find and circle the words. Write the missing letters.

femonsteriysouvenirmarainforestbcpostcardop

①  r_ _nfore_ _

②  s_ _ve_ _r

③  po_ _ca_ _

④  _ _n_ _er

2 Read and circle.

Garry is a teacher from Seattle, USA. On Sundays, he takes his backpack and his water bottle, and he goes to the Olympic National Park. He shows his students the trees and animals in the rainforest. The students draw pictures. He tells them stories about Bigfoot. The children aren't afraid of the monster because Garry's stories are funny.

1 Garry isn't an artist. He's a **teacher** / **reporter**.

2 Garry goes to the **park** / **rainforest** on Sundays.

3 Garry takes a water bottle and a **first aid kit** / **backpack**.

4 The children **draw pictures** / **take photos**.

5 Garry's stories about the **monster** / **animals** are funny.

Vocabulary rainforest, postcard, souvenirs, monster

1 Look, read, and write.

fashion   lunch   parade   shopping

①  ②  ③  ④

_____   _____   _____   _____

2 Read, look, and circle.

I'm Simon and I'm reporting from the Thanksgiving parade in New York City! It starts at nine o'clock in the morning and finishes at eleven thirty. It's very cold, but a lot of people are here watching it. They're wearing warm coats, scarves, and gloves. They can't go shopping today because the stores are closed. They go home for a big lunch!

1 Simon is a...

2 The parade starts at...

3 The people are...

4 The parade finishes at...

5 They're wearing...

6 People will go home for...

Summer Camp

1 Look, read, and match.

①  ②  ③  ④

graham crackers   marshmallows   month   summer camp

2 Read, look, and make a ✓ or an ✗.

Welcome to **Summer Camp Fun!**

These are our rules.

✓ Bring a water bottle and a backpack.

✓ Bring shoes like sneakers.

✓ Bring a sweater because it's cold at night.

✓ Wear sunglasses and a cap when it's sunny.

✗ Don't bring a first aid kit. There's one in the big tent.

✗ Don't play with the campfire. Cook your marshmallows on the fire, but remember: fires are dangerous for the forest.

Have fun, but take care of the forest and its animals.

①  ②

③   ④

⑤   ⑥

⑦   ⑧

OXFORD
UNIVERSITY PRESS

Great Clarendon Street, Oxford, OX2 6DP, United Kingdom

Oxford University Press is a department of the University of Oxford.
It furthers the University's objective of excellence in research, scholarship,
and education by publishing worldwide. Oxford is a registered trade
mark of Oxford University Press in the UK and in certain other countries

ISBN: 978 0 19 403366 4

Printed in China

This book is printed on paper from certified and well-managed sources

ACKNOWLEDGEMENTS

Back cover photograph: Oxford University Press building/David Fisher

Cover Image: Graham Alder/MM Studios

Illustrations by: Jacqui Davis/Advocate Art pp.3, 4, 10, 18, 24, 32, 38, 46,
52; Venitia Dean/Advocate Art pp.5 (children with sports equipment),
6 (skateboard), 8 (girls skateboarding), 9, 12 (people at school drama hall),
14 (artist on poster), 15 (reporter), 17 (objects), 20 (underwater scene),
22 (children at aquarium), 23 (crab), 25 (Tour de France scene), 27 (children
in ex. 1), 28 (boys on the beach), 31 (tables), 33 (children on catwalk),
34 (characters in ex. 2), 36 (children shopping), 41 (items in ex. 1), 42 (children
on the phone), 47 (children), 50 (boy painting and girl with guitar),
53 (shopping list), 54 (girl shopping), 56 (couple at the market), 59 (pizza),
60 (girl and boy), 63 (items in ex. 1); John Hallett pp.2 (calendar), 7 (heart rate),
8 (boys and girls), 14 (children in costumes), 16 (all items in ex. 2), 9 (children
with snow globe), 21 (sea creatures), 26 (family tree), 27 (children before
race), 29, 35 (items in ex. 2), 36 (girls with catalogue), 37 (girl), 41 (items in
ex. 2), 43, 50 (girls doing sports), 53 (supermarket counter), 56 (man and
boy at the market), 60 (hockey and football), 61 (people hiking), 62 (items
in ex. 1); Andrew Painter pp.2 (characters), 5 (children at the beach), 6 (all
items except for skateboard), 7 (doctor and soccer player), 11 (professions),
12 (children expressing emotions), 13, 15 (posters and headshots), 16 (all
items in ex. 1), 17 (characters), 19 (animals), 20 (sea creatures in aquarium),
21 (beach and ocean), 22 (aquarium map), 23 (sea creatures), 25 (objects),
26 (characters in ex. 1), 28 (children doing activities), 30, 31 (characters and
objects), 33 (clothes), 34 (characters in ex. 1), 35 (items in ex. 1), 37 (clothes and
body outline), 39, 40, 42 (children at the park), 44, 45, 47 (objects), 48, 49, 51,
54 (food), 55, 57, 58, 59 (girl and objects), 61 (items in ex. 1), 62 (reporter and
items in ex. 2), 63 (items in ex. 2); Natalie Smilie/Bright p.11 (theatre stage).

*The publishers would like to thank the following for permission to reproduce photographs
and other copyright material*: Graham Alder/MM Studios pp.14, 22; Shutterstock/
Darrin Henry p.9.